I0814618

King Cobra

by Julie Murray

Abdo Kids Jumbo is an Imprint of Abdo Kids
abdobooks.com

abdobooks.com

Published by Abdo Kids, a division of ABDO, P.O. Box 398166, Minneapolis, Minnesota 55439.
Copyright © 2025 by Abdo Consulting Group, Inc. International copyrights reserved in all countries. No part of this book may be reproduced in any form without written permission from the publisher. Abdo Kids Jumbo™ is a trademark and logo of Abdo Kids.

Printed in the United States of America, North Mankato, Minnesota.

102024

012025

Photo Credits: Getty Images, Minden Pictures, Science Source, Shutterstock

Production Contributors: Teddy Borth, Jennie Forsberg, Grace Hansen
Design Contributors: Candice Keimig, Pakou Moua

Library of Congress Control Number: 2024936623

Publisher's Cataloging-in-Publication Data

Names: Murray, Julie, author.

Title: King cobra / by Julie Murray

Description: Minneapolis, Minnesota : Abdo Kids, 2025 | Series: Royal animals | Includes online resources and index.

Identifiers: ISBN 9798384902973 (lib. bdg.) | ISBN 9798384903673 (ebook) | ISBN 9798384904021 (Read-to-me ebook)

Subjects: LCSH: King cobra--Juvenile literature. | Snakes--Juvenile literature. | Vipers--Juvenile literature. | Animal kingdom--Juvenile literature.

Classification: DDC 597.9642--dc23

Table of Contents

The King Cobra

The king cobra is a **venomous** snake that lives in Asia. It is found in forests, plains, and swamps. It often lives near a water source.

Asia
King
cobra
range
Indian
Ocean
Australia
N
W
E
S

The king cobra got its royal name for its large size and for what it eats. King cobras eat other cobras and snakes.

Body

The king cobra is the longest **venomous** snake in the world. It can reach lengths of more than 18 feet (5.5 m). It can weigh up to 20 pounds (9.1 kg)!

Adult king cobras are green, brown, or black in color. They have light markings. Their throats are light cream or yellow.

Deadly Bite

A king cobra can raise one-third of its body off the ground. It does this when it feels **threatened**. It can move forward in this position and follow its enemy.

To prepare for attack, the king cobra flattens its neck into a hood and hisses. Then, it lunges forward with a striking bite.

King cobras have sharp fangs and a **lethal** bite. They release **venom** into their **prey**. Their venom is deadly to humans and other animals.

Food

King cobras mainly eat other snakes. But they also eat lizards and small mammals. Like other snakes, king cobras have **flexible** jaws. They swallow their **prey** whole!

Baby King Cobras

King cobras are the only snakes that build nests for their eggs. Females lay 20 to 40 eggs at a time. They guard the nest until the eggs hatch.

More Facts

- King cobras are constantly growing. They shed their skin five times a year.
- After a large meal, king cobras can go for months without eating.
- The bite of a king cobra has enough venom to kill an elephant!

Glossary

flexible – easily bent without breaking.

lethal – deadly.

prey – an animal that is eaten by other animals.

threatened – to feel in danger.

venomous – producing a fluid, called venom, that is a poison to humans and animals.

Index

Visit **abdokids.com** to access crafts, games, videos, and more!

Use Abdo Kids code

RKK2973

or scan this QR code!